Creepy Castles

by Sarah Parvis

Consultant: Troy Taylor
President of the American Ghost Society

BEARPORT PUBLISHING

New York, New York

Credits

Cover and Title Page, © Andre Klaassen/istockphoto.com and © Rasmus Rasmussen/istockphoto.com; 4–5, © age fotostock/SuperStock; 6, © Sir Simon Marsden/The Marsden Archive/Alamy; 7, © Geomphotography/Alamy; 8, © Sir Simon Marsden/The Marsden Archive/Alamy; 8 (inset), © Imagno/Getty Images; 9, © The Granger Collection, New York; 10, © David Hunter/Robert Harding World Imagery/Corbis; 11, © Joel Sartore/Getty Images/National Geographic; 12, © The Granger Collection, New York; 13T, © Mary Evans Picture Library; 13B, © David Lyons/Alamy; 14, © Ronald Sumners/Shutterstock; 15T, © Kunisada, Utagawa (1786-1864)/Visual Arts Library (London)/Alamy; 15B, © J Marshall-Tribaleye Images/Alamy; 16, © Gail Johnson/Shutterstock; 17T, © Gina Goforth/Shutterstock; 17B, © Mary Evans Picture Library/Alamy; 18, © Jonathan Blair/National Geographic/Getty Images; 19, © Bettmann/CORBIS; 20, © BL Images Ltd/Alamy; 21, © Ian Beesley/Photonica/Getty Images; 22, © Aron Ellefson; 23T, © Erich Lessing/Art Resource, NY; 23B, © Vincent Giordano/Shutterstock; 24, © Chris Gibson/Alamy; 25, © Ingram Publishing/SuperStock; 26, © Vittoriano Rastelli/CORBIS; 27, © Photos 12/Alamy; 31, © Marek Szumlas/Shutterstock.

Publisher: Kenn Goin
Editorial Director: Adam Siegel
Creative Director: Spencer Brinker
Design: Dawn Beard Creative
Photo Researcher: Beaura Kathy Ringrose

Library of Congress Cataloging-in-Publication Data

Parvis, Sarah E.
Creepy castles / by Sarah Parvis; consultant, Troy Taylor.
p. cm. — (Scary places)
Includes bibliographical references and index.
ISBN-13: 978-1-59716-576-1 (library binding)
ISBN-10: 1-59716-576-X (library binding)
1. Castles—Juvenile literature. 2. Haunted places—Juvenile literature. I. Taylor, Troy. II. Title.

GT3550.P37 2008
940.1—dc22

2007038067

For more information, write to Bearport Publishing Company, Inc., 101 Fifth Avenue, Suite 6R, New York, New York, 10003. Printed in the United States of America.

10 9 8 7 6 5 4 3 2 1

10/08

Contents

Creepy Castles

What's the scariest thing about castles? Is it the **torture chamber** where prisoners were boiled in pots? Maybe it's the **dungeon** where victims were thrown into a pit filled with spikes. For some it's the mysterious ghosts that roam the empty hallways at night.

Whichever is most frightening, each scary scene is a reminder that deadly and spooky events often took place within a castle's thick stone walls. In the 11 creepy castles in this book, you'll meet the ghost of a queen who carries her head as she wanders, a **court jester** with a murderous sense of humor, a deadly drummer boy, and even a bloodsucking **vampire**, waiting to surprise her next victim.

Hidden Room of Death

Leap Castle, County Offaly, Ireland

The powerful O'Carroll **clan** lived at Leap Castle in the 1500s. These fierce fighters were often at war with other families. Many of their prisoners were killed in the castle's deadly dungeon. How exactly did they die? A fire would reveal the answer hundreds of years later.

Leap Castle

In 1922, a fire destroyed much of Leap Castle. As workers were cleaning up after the blaze, they made a terrifying discovery. Hidden beneath one of the floors was a secret dungeon. Sharp spikes came up from the stone floor. Hundreds of skeletons were still piled up inside.

To whom did the bones belong? Some were prisoners that the O'Carrolls had captured. Others were men hired to fight for the bloodthirsty clan. The O'Carrolls decided it was cheaper to murder the men after they were done fighting than to pay them. So they just threw them into the dungeon.

Prisoners thrown into Leap Castle's dungeon were lucky if they fell upon the spikes. At least they died quickly. Those who didn't land on spikes were trapped and forgotten, left to starve on top of a pile of rotting **corpses**.

The Bloodthirsty Ruler

Poienari Castle, Wallachia, Romania

Prince Vlad (1431–1476) had an unusual way of murdering his enemies. He pierced them with a sharp pole. The poles were then planted in the ground. Victims would hang in the air, slowly dying from their wounds. Anyone who came across the rows of **impaled** bodies would think twice about challenging this cruel ruler, who soon came to be known as Vlad the Impaler.

Poienari Castle

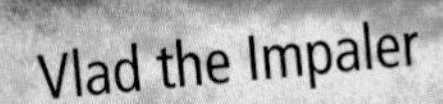

Vlad the Impaler

Vlad the Impaler was the prince of Wallachia, which is part of Romania. He needed a strong castle to keep him safe from his enemies. So Prince Vlad found a building that would be nearly impossible to attack—Poienari Castle. It was an ancient fortress located on a steep cliff in Romania. There was one problem, though. The castle lay in ruins. Prince Vlad would need many men to rebuild it. He knew just who to use.

Vlad's father and brother had been murdered in 1447. The noblemen who were supposed to defend his family did nothing to save them. As a punishment, Prince Vlad rounded up their families. He forced them to hike more than 50 miles (80 km) in the snow to his new castle. Those who survived the journey were put to work. They were forced to carry huge rocks for the castle walls. Many were worked to death. Those who lived were rewarded with a slow and painful death. Vlad impaled them on **stakes** around the castle.

Vlad's father was called *Vlad Dracul*, which means "Vlad the dragon" in Romanian. Prince Vlad was called *Vlad Dracula*, which means "Vlad, son of the dragon." Though he was not rumored to drink blood, Prince Vlad may have been the inspiration for the vampire in Bram Stoker's novel *Dracula* (1897).

Prince Vlad, surrounded by his victims, enjoys a meal.

A Murderous Marriage

Castle Rising, Norfolk, England

What happens when a queen is imprisoned in her own castle? Does she go mad? Does she turn into a ghostly wolf after her death? Or does she do both?

Queen Isabella was only about 12 years old when she married King Edward II of England in 1308. It was not a marriage that would last, however. After 17 years, Queen Isabella fell in love with Roger Mortimer. Together, they gathered up an army, captured King Edward II, and had him killed on September 21, 1327.

Castle Rising

Isabella and Edward's son, Edward III, became the new king. According to some, Edward III let his mother live the rest of her life in peace. Others, however, tell a different tale. They believe Edward III punished Isabella by sending her away to Castle Rising. There, she spent almost 30 years locked away from the world. Some stories say she went completely mad. To this day, visitors to Castle Rising have heard her crazed laughter echoing through the courtyards. Some have even seen her ghost. It takes the form of a giant white wolf with bloody fangs and fiery red eyes.

Queen Isabella may not be the only noisy ghost in the family. The ghost of King Edward II is heard every year on the day of his painful murder. His piercing screams fill the hallways of Berkeley Castle in Gloucestershire, England, where he was killed.

A Phantom Prankster

Muncaster Castle, Cumbria, England

Kings, queens, and other powerful people had servants to do everything for them. They had cooks to prepare food and messengers to carry letters. They even had a person whose job was to make them laugh! This court jester, or fool, would juggle, dance, play music, tell jokes, and play pranks to entertain his master. At Muncaster Castle, one court jester kept playing tricks even after he died.

Archaeologist Clifford Jones went to Muncaster Castle in 2002 to look for ancient Roman coins and pottery. Instead, he found the ghost of Tom Fool—a court jester who lived about 400 years ago.

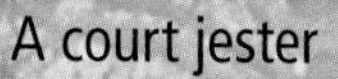

A court jester

A person trapped in quicksand

Tom was an expert at playing tricks on people. Sometimes travelers would come to the castle and ask for directions to London. If Tom did not like them, he would point them not toward the city but toward deadly **quicksand**. Who knows how many travelers were buried alive because of Tom's wicked jokes?

Some people, including Clifford Jones, believe that Tom continues to make **mischief** from beyond the **grave**. One night, Clifford heard eerie chopping sounds in the empty castle. He asked Tom's ghost to stop. Suddenly, it was quiet. A moment later, a lightbulb above him exploded. Clifford turned the corner and another bulb blew up. Everywhere he went, the lights shattered until he fled, hoping Tom Fool would not follow.

Muncaster Castle

Sir Pennington was Tom Fool's master. He, too, could be cruel. He wanted to punish a local carpenter for falling in love with his daughter. So he ordered Tom to murder the young man. Tom did just that. He cut off his head.

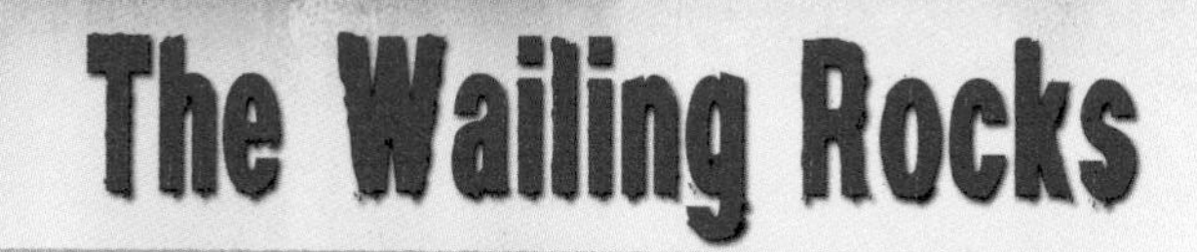

The Wailing Rocks

Hachioji Castle, Tokyo, Japan

Castles often had large armies to protect the men and women living inside. A tricky enemy, however, might wait to attack until an army was not around. What could the helpless people trapped inside do? More than 400 years ago, the Japanese women living at Hachioji Castle found out the sad answer.

A samurai on horseback

Hachioji Castle was built by the Japanese warrior Hojo Ujiteru in 1570. It stood for just 20 years before **tragedy** struck. On June 23, 1590, an army of fierce **samurai** led by Lord Toyotomi Hideyoshi attacked the castle. Unfortunately, there weren't many warriors to defend the building. Most of Hojo Ujiteru's forces were away fighting in a different battle. The women who remained at the castle knew they would not be safe for long.

To avoid being captured and tortured, the women jumped to their deaths from the top of Hachioji Castle. It is said that their bodies created waterfalls of blood on the rocks below. The samurai destroyed much of the castle that day. Since then, it has remained **abandoned**, haunted by the doomed women. Visitors to the ruins report hearing the spine-chilling screams of women. They also hear the sickening thuds of bodies hitting the rocks.

According to Japanese tradition, the ghosts of people who were murdered or who killed themselves are not able to rest peacefully. They remain on Earth seeking revenge. People should be very careful if they leave their homes between 2:00 and 3:00 A.M. This is the time when these ghosts are most active.

The Blue Boy

Chillingham Castle, Northumberland, England

During the 1200s, up to 50 people a week were tortured at Chillingham Castle. So it's no surprise that this building is said to be haunted by its bloody past. One of its most well-known ghosts is the mysterious Blue Boy.

Chillingham Castle

Chillingham Castle was built in the 1100s. Today, tourists can stay overnight in some parts of the haunted castle. Beware of sleeping in the Pink Room, however. That is where the ghostly Blue Boy appears.

Those who have slept in the Pink Room say that the Blue Boy shows up at midnight. At that hour they hear a blood-curdling wail. It sounds like the awful cry of a child in great pain. When the startled guests look up, the image of a boy dressed in blue appears. He is surrounded by a glowing light. The ghost stays for a moment, then floats toward the fireplace and disappears through a wall.

In the 1920s, bones and scraps of blue clothing were found hidden behind the wall where the ghostly boy vanishes. Perhaps they belonged to him. The bones were given a proper burial in the hope of finally giving the boy's spirit some rest. So far it hasn't worked.

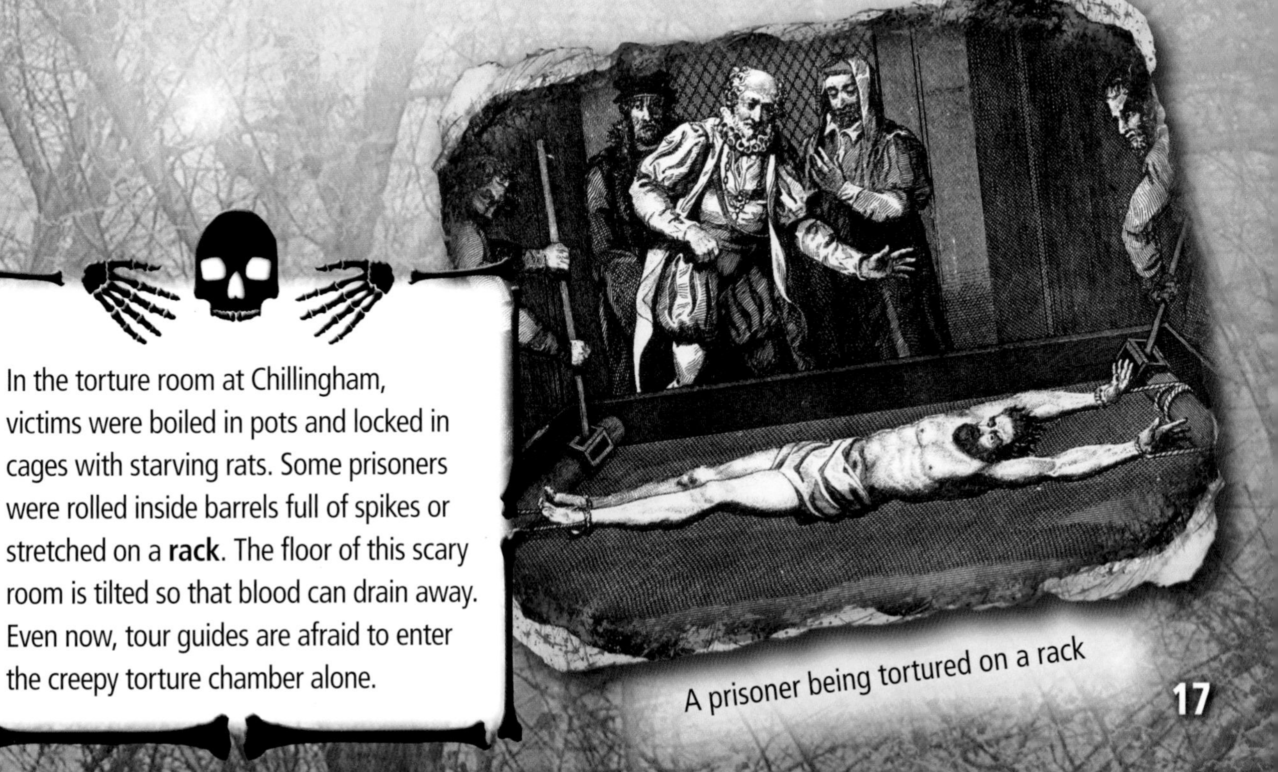

In the torture room at Chillingham, victims were boiled in pots and locked in cages with starving rats. Some prisoners were rolled inside barrels full of spikes or stretched on a **rack**. The floor of this scary room is tilted so that blood can drain away. Even now, tour guides are afraid to enter the creepy torture chamber alone.

A prisoner being tortured on a rack

The Headless Queen

Tower of London, London, England

The Tower of London has been used as both a fortress and a home to England's kings and queens. It was also a famous jail. For hundreds of years, prisoners at the Tower of London were tortured, **beheaded**, hanged, and burned at the stake. With so many violent deaths, it's no wonder that some say the Tower is the most haunted castle in England.

The Tower of London

King Henry VIII ruled England from 1509 to 1547. He married his second wife, Anne Boleyn, in 1533. Together, they lived at the Tower of London. King Henry hoped they would have a son who would become king after him. When Anne did not have a boy, King Henry began to lose interest in her. He wanted to marry another woman who would give him a son. So in 1536 he imprisioned Anne in the Tower and sentenced her to death.

On May 19, 1536, Anne stepped onto a small platform on the Tower's lawn. She gave a short speech before kneeling down. A blindfold was tied around her face so she could not see what was coming next. With one blow, a swordsman sliced off her head. She was then buried in an unmarked grave.

Yet some people say the queen can still be seen. Her headless ghost is said to roam around the Tower. Sometimes she even carries her head as she wanders.

Anne Boleyn about to be killed

Anne Boleyn was lucky to be killed with a sword. Most beheadings took place with an ax. If the ax was not sharp enough or if the **executioner** had poor aim, the victim would not die instantly. In 1541, Margaret Pole, the Countess of Salisbury, was struck many times with an ax before she died.

A Watery Grave

Scotney Castle, Kent, England

One way to keep a castle safe was to build a **moat** around it. This deep ditch filled with water made it very difficult for attackers to reach the people in a castle. Many castles had moats. Some were even said to be the home of ghosts.

Scotney Castle

Scotney Castle, built in the 1300s, is located in Kent, England. In the 1700s, England was home to many **smugglers**. Some sold illegal items. Others sold items without paying **taxes** to the king. The smugglers had to be careful. If they were caught, they could be killed.

Arthur Darell owned Scotney Castle in the early 1700s. It is said that he was a smuggler—and probably a murderer, too. According to local stories, when an officer discovered that Darell was a smuggler, the two men began to fight. Darell killed the officer and dumped the body into the moat at Scotney Castle so he would not be caught. Ever since, people have reported seeing a dripping wet ghost crawling out of the water. It limps slowly to the castle. The ghost bangs on the door, but no sounds can be heard. Then the figure disappears into thin air.

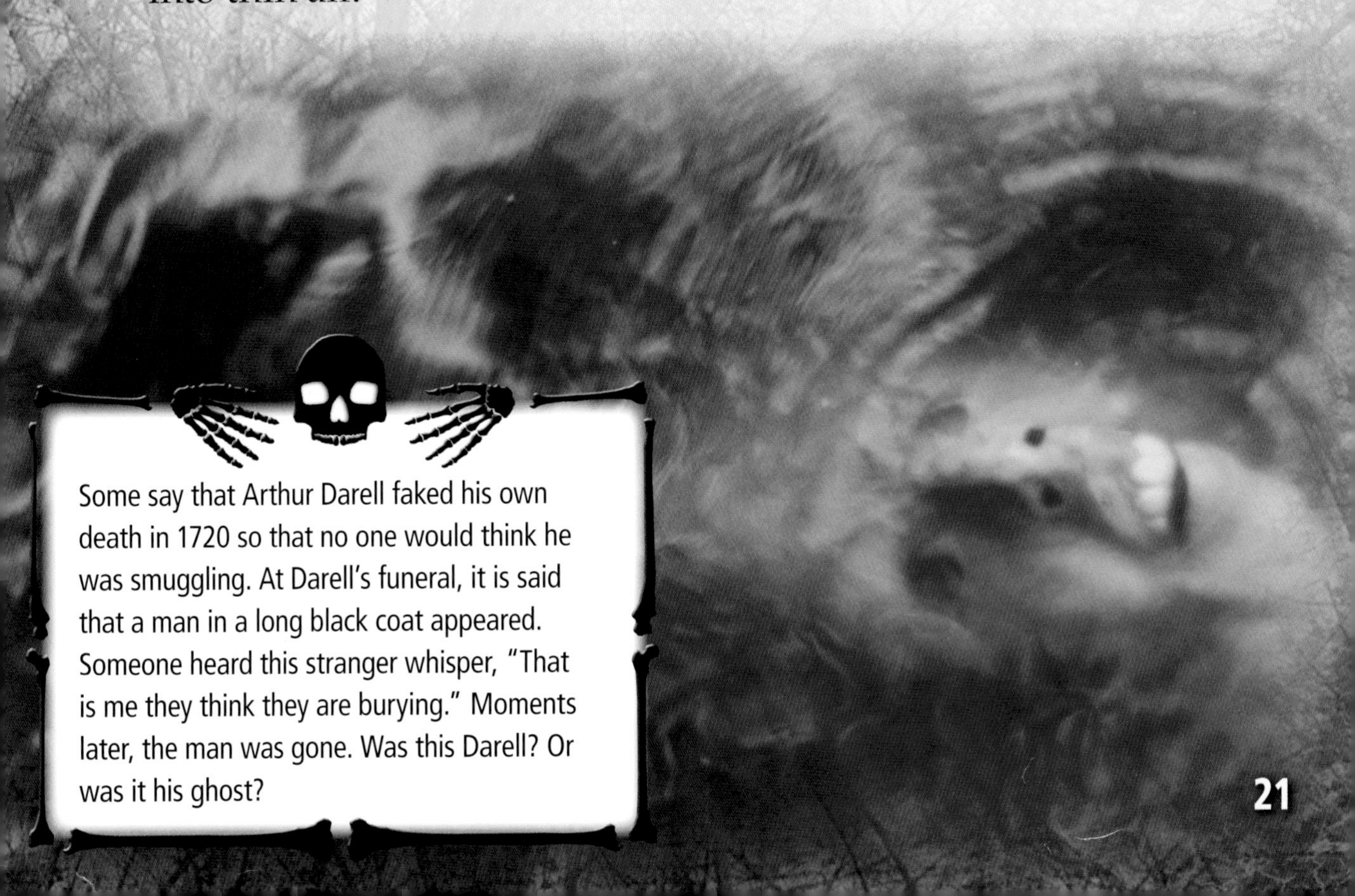

Some say that Arthur Darell faked his own death in 1720 so that no one would think he was smuggling. At Darell's funeral, it is said that a man in a long black coat appeared. Someone heard this stranger whisper, "That is me they think they are burying." Moments later, the man was gone. Was this Darell? Or was it his ghost?

The Deadly Drummer Boy

Cortachy Castle, Angus, Scotland

Is it possible to know when a person will die? According to Scottish **folklore**, it is. Just listen for the sound of the **banshee**. Some people believe that hearing the wails of this ghostly woman outside a house means that a person inside will soon die. Scotland's Cortachy Castle, however, has its own messenger of death—a ghostly drummer boy.

Cortachy Castle

During the 1800s, members of the Ogilvy family often lived in fear. Their home, Cortachy Castle, was haunted by a ghostly drummer boy. Whenever his deadly playing was heard, a member of the Ogilvy household would soon die. David Ogilvy, **Earl** of Airlie, is one family member who wished he'd never heard the drumming. In 1835, the earl heard the ghostly drummer boy. Soon after, his wife died.

Three years later, David Ogilvy married another woman, Margaret Bruce. In 1845, a guest was visiting the castle. She heard the sound of drumming coming from below her window. It seemed like it filled the whole building. When she asked about the drumming, the earl and his second wife turned pale. They could not escape the curse placed on their castle. Within months, the earl's second wife was dead.

There are several stories about how the drummer boy had died. Most say he was a young man who had worked for the Ogilvys during the **Middle Ages**. One day, his master became so angry with him that he threw the boy from a window high in the castle. Some say he was stuffed into his drum before being thrown to his death.

A Museum Mystery

Tamworth Castle, Staffordshire, England

Tamworth Castle, part of which is now a museum, was built in the late 1000s. Today, tourists can visit different parts of the building, including its dungeon and haunted bedroom. The men and women who work at Tamworth say that ghostly figures are often spotted around the castle. Sounds sometimes come from empty rooms. Even recently, workers have seen—and felt—things that they cannot explain.

Tamworth Castle

In the 1990s, a museum worker named June Hall was preparing an **exhibit** for the castle called "The Tamworth Story." When she opened up the exhibit room one morning, she felt as if sand had been thrown in her face.

For a moment, June was blinded. She looked down, thinking she would be covered in dirt. Yet her clothes were clean. Val Lee, another member of the staff, entered the room just then. She saw June bent over, rubbing her eyes. When they both looked up, they did not see a person. Instead, they saw a swirl of blue mist. It was six feet (2 m) tall. Then, as quickly as it had appeared, the mist was gone.

Neither June nor Val knows what could have caused these spooky events. Was it one of the many ghosts that live at Tamworth Castle?

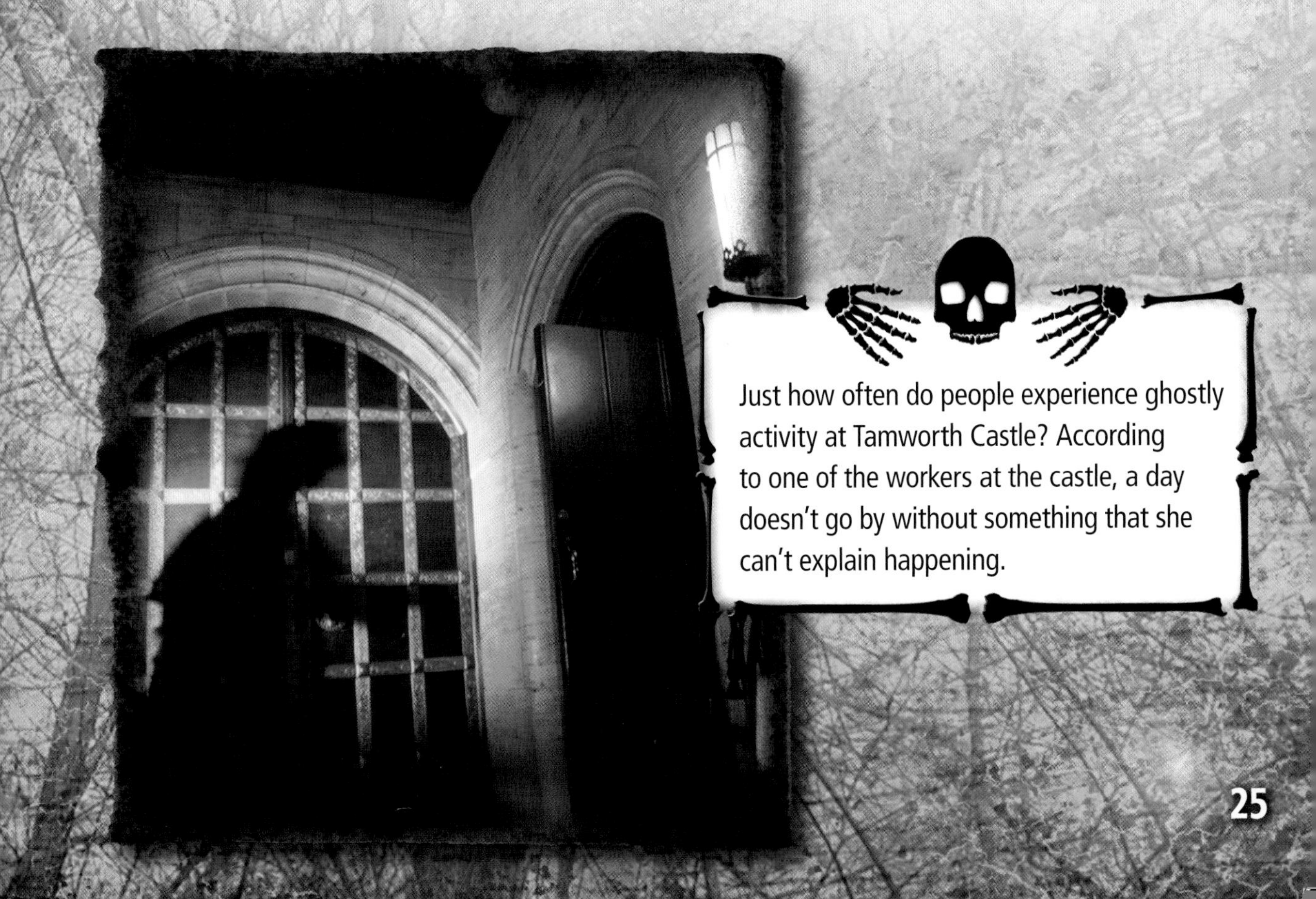

Just how often do people experience ghostly activity at Tamworth Castle? According to one of the workers at the castle, a day doesn't go by without something that she can't explain happening.

The Hidden Vampire

Glamis Castle, Angus, Scotland

There are many creepy castles in Scotland, but Glamis Castle may be the spookiest. It is said to be the home of several unusual guests, including a vampire. Vampires are dead people who rise from their graves at night to suck the blood of the living. Unfortunately, these creatures are also very hard to destroy, as the owners of Glamis found out.

Glamis Castle

People began building Glamis Castle in the 1400s. Some say that in its early years, the castle's owners found out a shocking secret about one of their servants. She was a vampire! They made this discovery when the young servant girl was caught sucking the blood from one of her victims. To protect themselves, her terrified masters threw the vampire into a small room. It was sealed so she could not escape. With no food and water, she was left to die. Yet some say she still lives.

According to **legend**, there are only a few ways to kill a vampire. The vampire must be left in the sunlight, or a wooden stake must be driven through its heart. A person can also kill one of these monsters by cutting off its head or burning its body. Since the vampire of Glamis was simply locked away, some believe she is still alive in her secret room. There she sits, waiting to be discovered, so that she can continue her bloodsucking ways.

Lady Janet Douglas lived at Glamis Castle in the 1500s. Falsely accused of being a witch, she was burned at the stake in 1537. Since that time, people have often claimed to see her ghost. Some say it has a red glow, as if surrounded by flames.

Female vampire

Creepy Castles

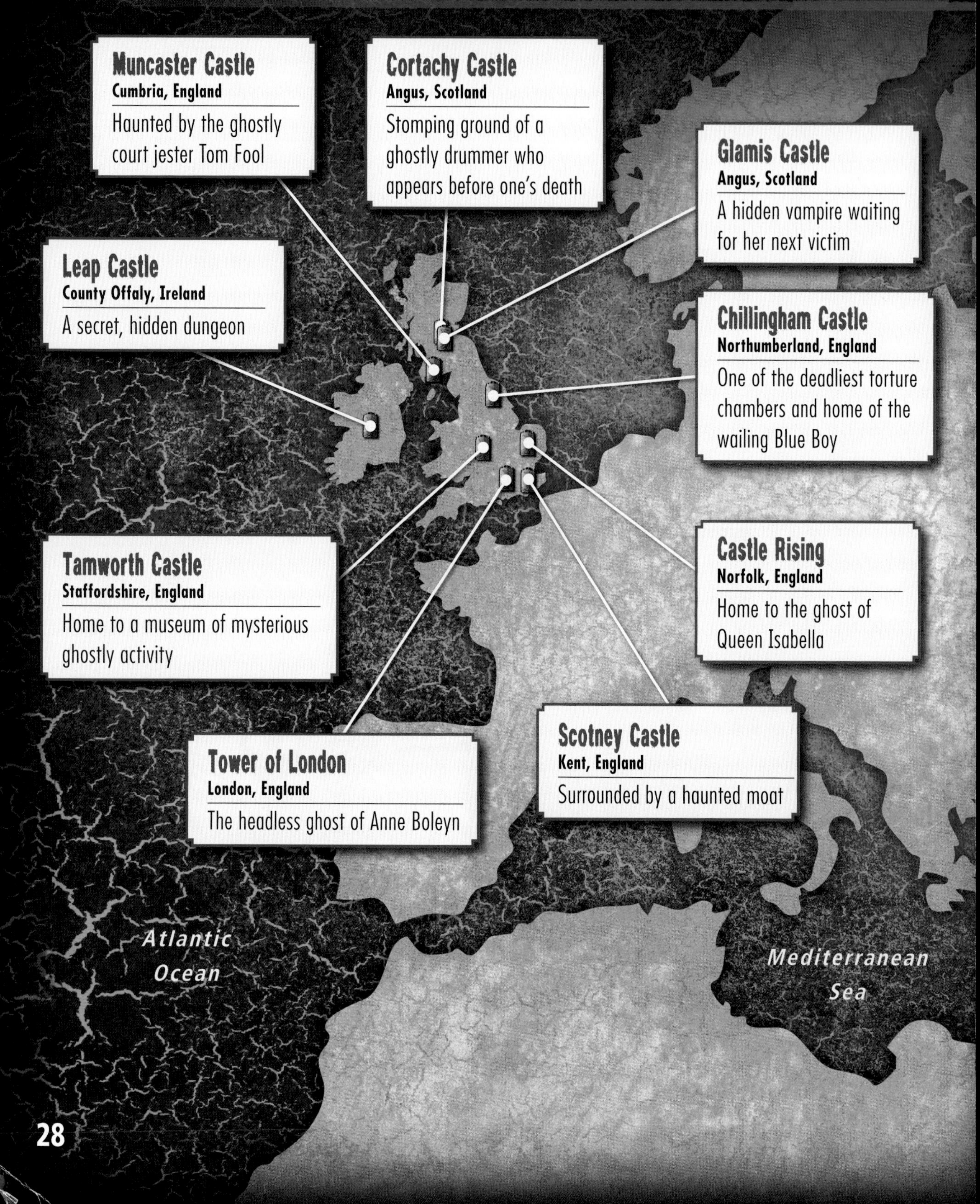

Muncaster Castle
Cumbria, England
Haunted by the ghostly court jester Tom Fool

Cortachy Castle
Angus, Scotland
Stomping ground of a ghostly drummer who appears before one's death

Glamis Castle
Angus, Scotland
A hidden vampire waiting for her next victim

Leap Castle
County Offaly, Ireland
A secret, hidden dungeon

Chillingham Castle
Northumberland, England
One of the deadliest torture chambers and home of the wailing Blue Boy

Tamworth Castle
Staffordshire, England
Home to a museum of mysterious ghostly activity

Castle Rising
Norfolk, England
Home to the ghost of Queen Isabella

Scotney Castle
Kent, England
Surrounded by a haunted moat

Tower of London
London, England
The headless ghost of Anne Boleyn

Atlantic Ocean

Mediterranean Sea

Around the World

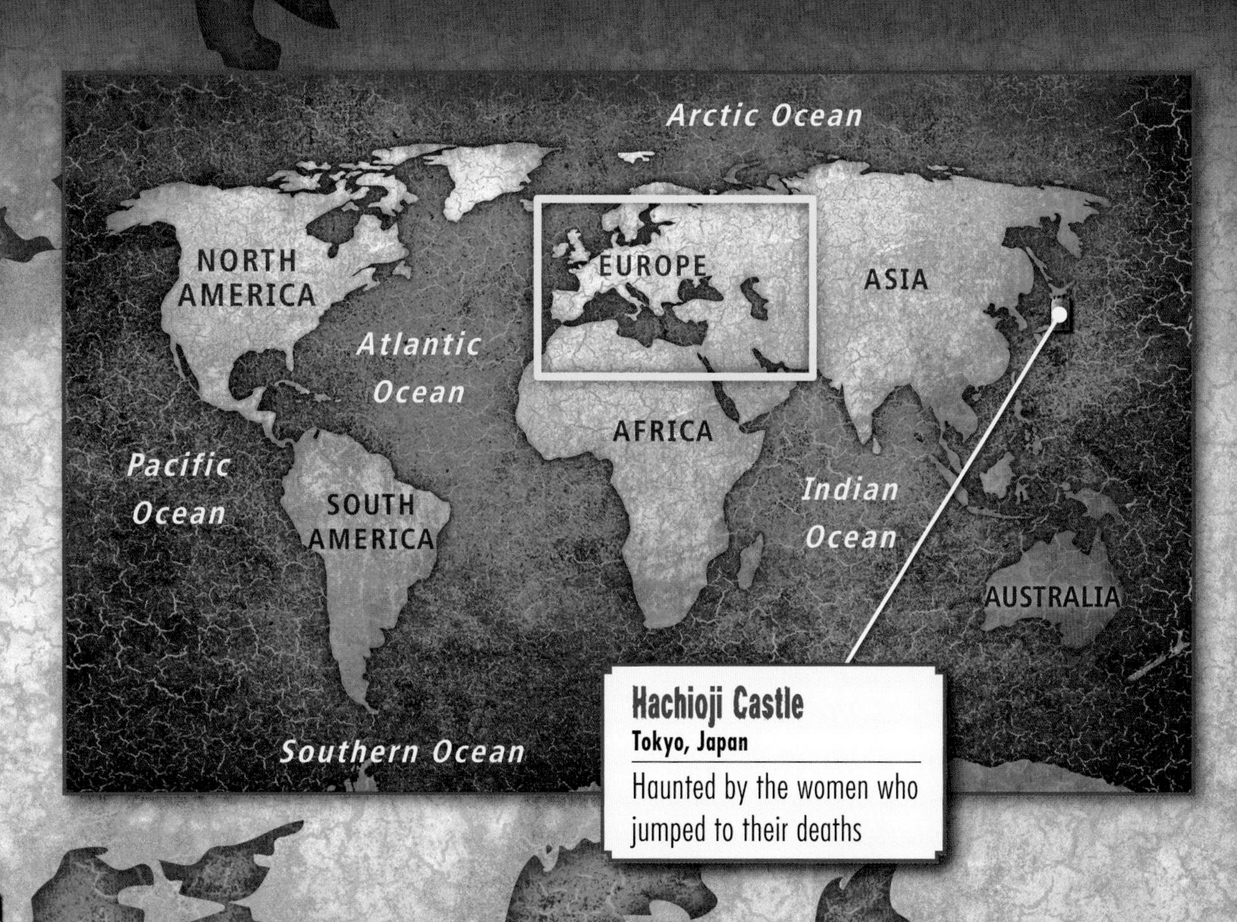

Hachioji Castle
Tokyo, Japan
Haunted by the women who jumped to their deaths

Poienari Castle
Wallachia, Romania
Fortress of the cruel ruler, Vlad the Impaler

Glossary

abandoned (uh-BAN-duhnd) left empty; no longer used

archaeologist (*ar*-kee-OL-uh-jist) a scientist who learns about ancient times by studying things he or she digs up, such as old buildings, tools, and pottery

banshee (BAN-shee) the wailing spirit of a woman who is seen or heard when a person is about to die

beheaded (bi-HED-id) had one's head chopped off

clan (KLAN) a large family or group of families with a single leader

corpses (KORPS-iz) dead bodies

court jester (KORT JES-tur) a person whose job was to entertain kings, queens, and nobles in the Middle Ages (A.D. 400–1500)

dungeon (DUHN-juhn) a dark prison cell, usually underground

earl (URL) a British nobleman

executioner (*ek*-suh-KYOO-shuh-ner) a person whose job is to kill prisoners

exhibit (eg-ZIB-it) a presentation or display; something that is shown to many people

folklore (FOHK-*lor*) the stories and beliefs of a group of people

grave (GRAYV) a hole dug into the ground where a dead person is buried

impaled (im-PAYLD) killed by being stabbed with a sharp pole

legend (LEJ-uhnd) a story handed down from long ago that is often based on some facts but cannot be proven true

Middle Ages (MID-uhl AJE-iz) a time period in European history from about A.D. 400 to around 1500

mischief (MISS-chif) playing pranks or doing things to annoy others

moat (MOHT) a wide ditch dug around a palace or castle that is filled with water

quicksand (KWIK-sand) wet, loose sand that someone can sink into and become stuck

rack (RAK) a rectangular torture device on which a person's body is stretched in order to cause great pain

samurai (SAM-oo-*rye*) Japanese warriors, or soldiers, who lived in medieval times (A.D. 400–1500)

smugglers (SMUHG-lurz) people who secretly bring in or take out goods in a way that is against the law

stakes (STAYKS) strong sticks or poles with a pointed end

taxes (TAKS-iz) money people pay to support the government

torture chamber (TOR-chur CHAYM-bur) a room where someone causes great pain to another

tragedy (TRAJ-uh-dee) a terrible event that causes great sadness or suffering

vampire (VAM-*pye*-ur) in stories, a dead person who rises from the grave to suck the blood of people

Bibliography

Belanger, Jeff, ed. *Encyclopedia of Haunted Places: Ghostly Locales from Around the World.* Franklin Lakes, NJ: New Page Books (2005).

Coulombe, Charles A. *Haunted Castles of the World: Ghostly Legends and Phenomena from Keeps and Fortresses Around the Globe.* Guilford, CT: The Lyons Press (2004).

Jones, Richard. *Haunted Castles of Britain and Ireland.* New York: Barnes & Noble (2003).

Marsden, Simon. *This Spectred Isle: A Journey Through Haunted England.* New York: Barnes & Noble (2005).

Whitaker, Terence. *Haunted England: Royal Spirits, Castle Ghosts, Phantom Coaches, & Wailing Ghouls.* Chicago: Contemporary Books, Inc. (1987).

Read More

Banks, Cameron. *Ghostly Graveyards and Spooky Spots.* New York: Scholastic (2003).

Gravett, Christopher. *Castle* (*DK Eyewitness Series*). New York: DK Publishing (2004).

Steele, Philip. *The World of Castles.* Boston: Kingfisher (2005).

Learn More Online

To learn more about creepy castles, visit
www.bearportpublishing.com/ScaryPlaces

Index

About the Author

Sarah Parvis is a writer and editor in New York. She lives in Brooklyn and loves ghost stories.